Published in the UK in 2025 by Post Wave Children's Books,
an imprint of Post Wave Publishing UK Ltd,
Runway East, 24-28 Bloomsbury Way, London, WC1A 2SN
www.postwavepublishing.com

First edition 2023
Published with permission of La Martinière Jeunesse
Original title: *J'ai Soif!*
Written and illustrated by Joanna Rzezak
Copyright © La Martinière Jeunesse,
une marque des Éditions de La Martinière,
57 rue Gaston Tessier, 75019 Paris, France, 2023

A catalogue record of this book is available from the British Library.

All rights reserved, including the right of reproduction
in whole or in part in any form.

10 9 8 7 6 5 4 3 2 1

ISBN: 978-1-83627-021-8

Printed in China

Joanna Rzezak

THE VERY LAST DROP!

Meet the Animals at the Waterhole

post wave

Across the African savannah, the sun begins to rise. The waterhole is already buzzing with activity. A bloat of hippopotamuses splashes about, enjoying their morning bath. Hungry crocodiles keep their eyes peeled for prey. They're ready to snap up breakfast!

As the sun beats down, the waterhole starts to warm up. Soon, the hippopotamuses' backs start to peek out of the pool. But why are they green?

Two big birds swoop down for a snack. The secretarybird lands first, stomping the ground with his long legs, searching for lizards and snakes. Nearby, the great blue heron stands as still as a statue, eyes fixed on the water. Then, with a SNAP, he gobbles up a fish!

Who is next in line at the waterhole?

It's the kudus! These graceful antelopes with their twirly horns can leap as high as three metres into the air! But just as they are about to take a drink . . .

Hey, I was here before you, kudu!

At midday, the blazing sun reaches its peak. Oryx, red hartebeest, impalas, guinea fowl and giraffes have all gathered here to cool down.

Even three Kirk's dik-diks have arrived. These timid little antelopes are only the size of a small dog, but they are not easy prey! When they sense danger, they freeze, then sprint for their lives at the last moment!

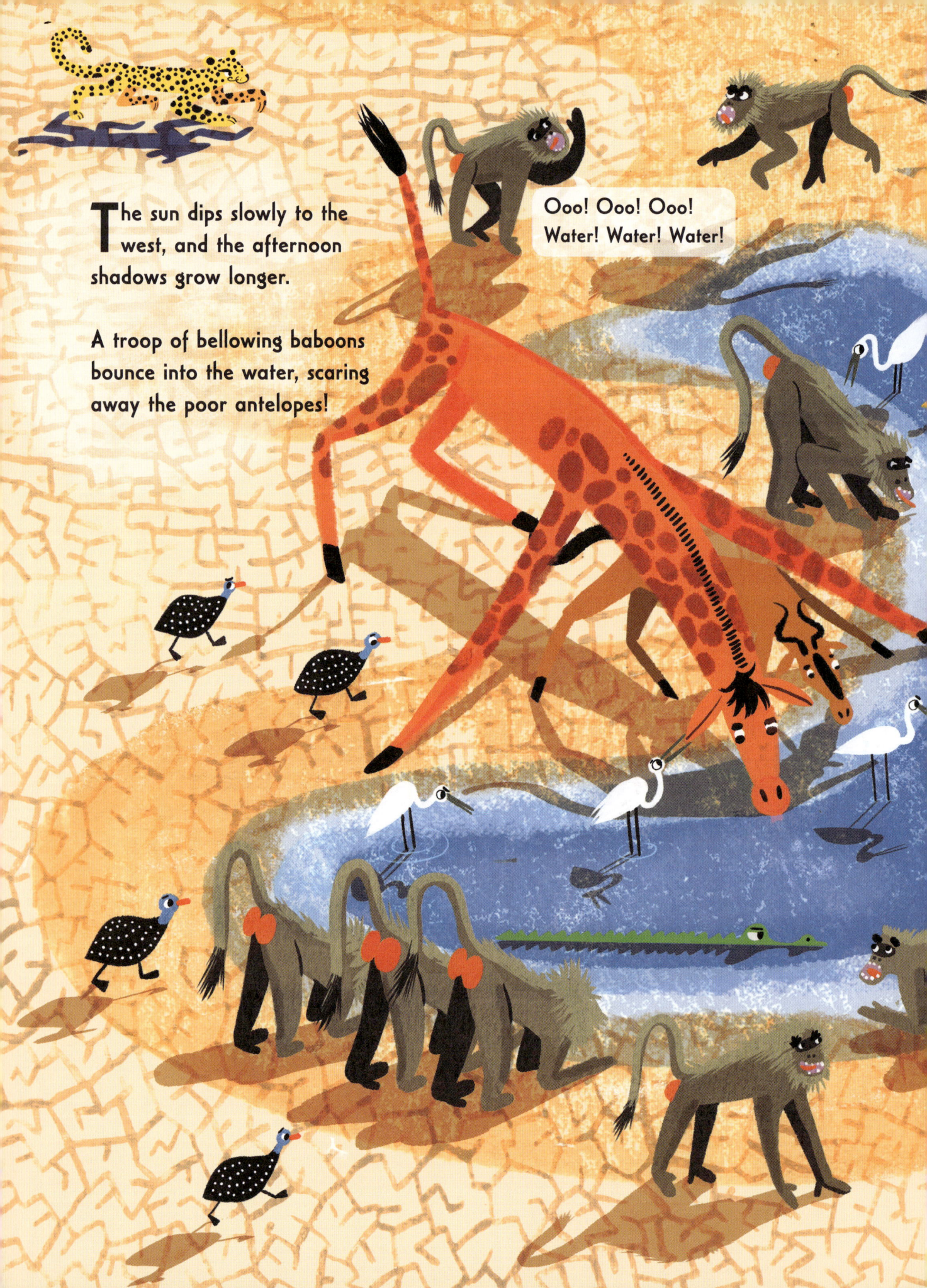

As the sun sets and the day comes to an end, a lone white rhinoceros slowly approaches the waterhole. She moves quietly, taking a gentle sip of the last drop of water. She is one of the last of her kind – her great, beautiful horns making her a target for hunters.

Oh, poor ostrich! She has finally made her way back to the waterhole, but it's too late. There's not a single drop of water left! With a heavy heart, she realises she'll have to find somewhere else to quench her thirst.

A new day dawns. A thirsty little elephant begins to dig around the dried-up waterhole with her trunk and tusks. What is she doing?

She digs and digs until . . . she uncovers a new source of water, buried deep beneath the ground!

With a triumphant trumpet, she calls out, inviting all the other animals to return for a drink.

The waterhole is ready for another hot day on the savannah.

Save Every Drop!

Water is very important for all living things on Earth, but our planet is getting drier. Droughts are happening more often, and this means rivers are drying up, making it harder for animals and people to find enough water.

This problem used to mostly affect dry places, but now it's spreading because our planet's climate is changing.

This means our weather is shifting, with hotter temperatures and less rain in many areas. But, we can all make a difference and help to reverse this. By making small changes every day, we can protect this precious resource and ensure there's enough water for everyone.

Here are some useful things to try:

Take a shower rather than a bath. A shower uses up to four times less water than a single bath.

When showering, make sure that the water is turned off when you are lathering up and only turn it on to rinse off.

Turn the tap off when you are brushing your teeth.

Collect rainwater or cooking water for your plants instead of using a hose.

Shorten your shower time by using a playlist. Start washing with the first song, rinse during the next and be ready to hop out by the last one.

Don't leave the tap running when washing your face. Instead, you can use a wet flannel to scrub your face clean.

Water yout plants in the evening when it is cooler to stop the water evaporating before it reaches the soil.

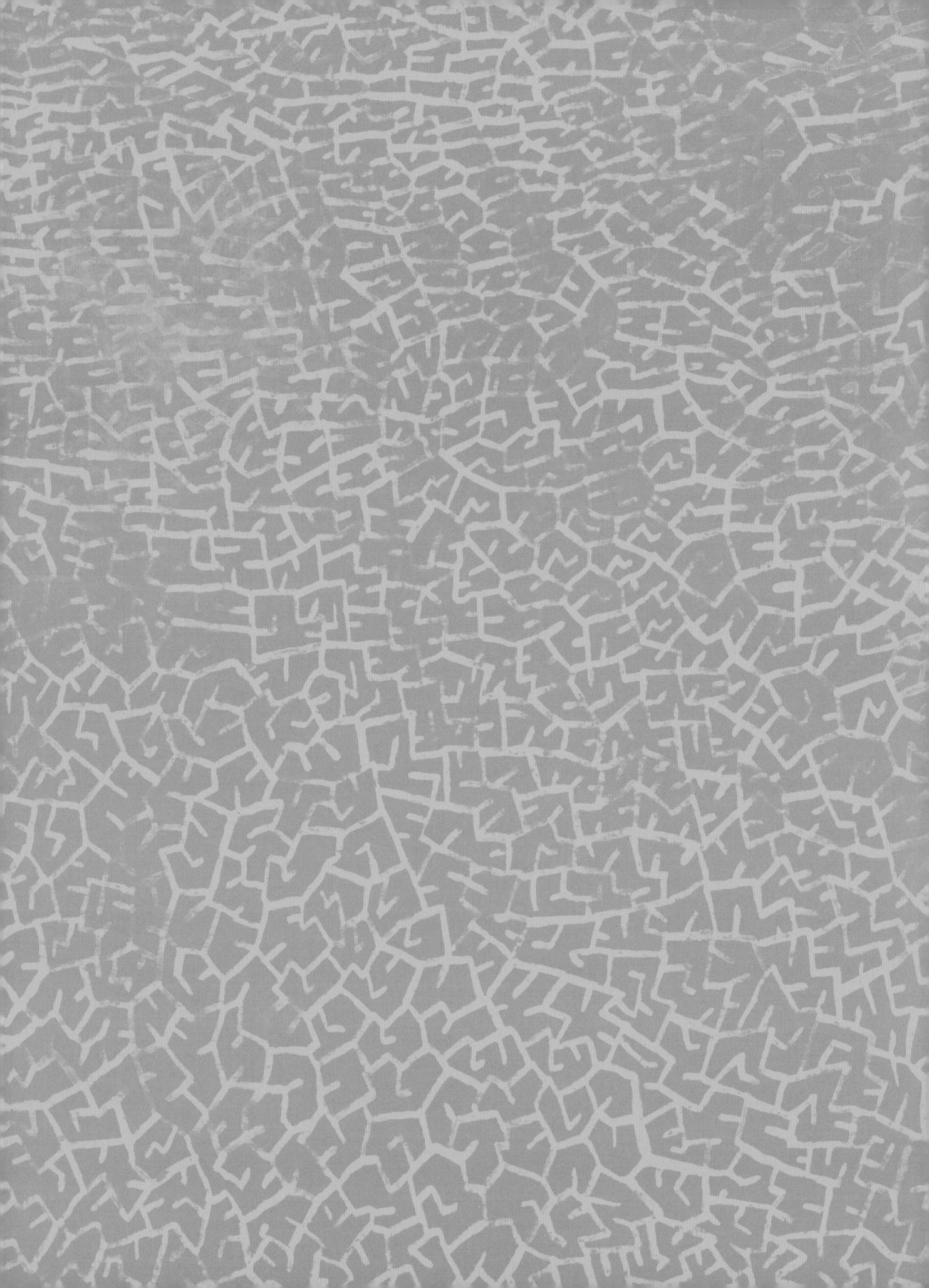